WINTER BARLEY

for Christine

WINTER BARLEY

George Gunn

CHAPMAN PUBLISHING

2005

Chapman Publishing
4 Broughton Place
Edinburgh EH1 3RX
Scotland

First published 2005

This book is published with the assistance of
the Scottish Arts Council Writers Factory Fund

A catalogue record for this volume is
available from the British Library
ISBN 1-903700-12-4

Chapman New Writing Series
Editor Joy Hendry
ISSN 0953-5306

Some of these poems have been previously featured in
*BBC Radio 4, BBC Radio Scotland, Breaking New Ground, Chapman,
The Dark Horse, The Edinburgh Review, New Writing Scotland,
SAC for Walter Cairns Anthology, Scotia Review,
Scottish Parliament Anthology* and *Poetry Scotland*

Cover and Design by Tom Bee

Printed by ARC colourprint ltd
12a Bonnington Lane, Edinburgh, EH6 5BJ

Contents

Dunnet 2000

They've built a house in Miller's field
they've built a house on my father's
damp three-quarter-acre
Dunnet lay once a crofting townland
of potato park & hayfield
a row of council houses & a shop
the kirk & pub confronting each other
like boxers locked in an exhausted embrace
with only a dry-stane dyke as referee
ringside to that was Lyall's farm
where every five o clock I'd bring the milk tin
my nostrils clotted in the sweet warm waft
of sharn & Atlantic silage
cropped from a dunescape of surf & salmon net

Rune Stations

To struggle with the parish pump
& put form to its ungainly gurgle
that is a stone cut rune
to carve a space in urban indifference
& pin our lyric proclamations to their door
that is a stone cut rune

to watch the dawn sweep over
a flat grey horizon
that is a stone cut rune
to put your mark
on the morning's silence
that is a stone cut rune

to organise those who will always refuse you
& then cry that they only know neglect
that is a stone cut rune
to mint the lead coinage of the dead
& see it spent on accusations
that is a stone cut rune

to feel the days sail by
like a hungry fishing fleet
that is a stone cut rune
to see starlight make golden
the base clay of mediocrity
that is a stone cut rune

to hear voices in your home
speak words which are not theirs
that is a stone cut rune
to comply in this ugly mimic
without knowing what you do
that is a stone cut rune

to lift the flagstone of memory
& count the missing fossils
that is a stone cut rune
to wrap your story
in the short mile of newsprint
that is a stone cut rune

to fish for meaning
in the sea of the air
that is a stone cut rune
to do all of this
& still leave room for wonder
that is a stone cut rune

The Central Hotel

The boys are searching for the men
who are sleeping deep inside of them
in groups they stand around the bar
like fields of winter barley

& drag their voices behind them like sea-ploughs
as if the search invites them to sleep
& the sound from their throats
could turn the fields of their tongues

what would they do if the sky embraced them
like smoke from a Spring hill-fire
& gave them that carbon-scarred urgency
for new growth & took them like some coughing guide

deep into the underworld of possibility?
The bar would tremble like the petal of an orchid
in the yawning dawn of a north coast morning
in a country that is looking for time

through the obvious jeopardy of one minute to the next
solutions form & complete themselves
as if they were milk dancing into cheese
Oh, I would guard the ancient wreck site

of this moment against any well-equipped diver
however beautiful or well-intentioned
I would carve runes on the oxidising anchor
what is this temptation of nothing

which raises voices & glazes eyes
& makes words ascend like crippled angels?
Is it because there is never enough silence
or perfume or the green rain of meaning?

The boys in the bar have problems
the size of red Atlantic sea-cliffs
& solutions as small as the generous
warmth of a human palm

in this they plant themselves like potatoes
or cupola rows of neeps
like crops against the storm
& fertilise the savage mould of circumstance

in their harvest of winter barley
in their sleeping search
in the bar of the Central hotel
by the grey argument of the firth

Ode to the Coming Summer

For PB

The coming Summer swims across the North
& breathes a cool May into an eager June
to coax the growth from beneath the earth

so the little heat can come & soon
the barley will green the ochre of the park
& the thrushes trill their grateful tune

in dawnings that shed the need for dark
& swallows can execute their figure eight
gathering up their strength to put the spark

of joy back into the fibre of their fate
which is to be the season's crowning glory
nothing is too early, nothing is too late

it is the Summer coming, neither sad nor sorry
giver & builder; this is her story

the sky may be grey but there is no need for tears
like the promise of an open hand
the season is a warning & a welcome of fears

which can be nourished across the land
cultivated in kind & hopeful furrows
& turned to warmth as nature planned

for we have no need of the weed of sorrows
the living bloom across the field is spread
& defies the desperate & the doomed to their burrows

to play endless dice with the dead
a game that needs neither sloth nor slurry
for the colour of life is constant red

& Summer has a mind it's time to marry
the blue space for birth; this is your story

a perfect pibroch from the Pentland Firth
summer circles the ever-moving shoal of meaning
days stretch & meld the myrtle of their mirth

from Hoy's high sandstone shelf, leaning
their elbows on Morven's accommodating prow,
to the velvet slipper of Kildonan's dreaming

in her hill-locked cradle where now
the acres are aggregated in a computer's bleep
the days caress the wrinkles on the brow

of history which is the subject of Kildonan's sleep
this northern landscape of calm and fury
where action & reaction are twenty feet deep

on the soft nether-bedrock of nitrogen & slurry
sweet Summer music; this is your story

if I were a deer made from rays of light
I would run with you across the hill
& splash through burns from day to night

& never stop my itchy running until
I had come to the high mountains of Kashmir
& broken out your bright crayons of creation & filled

the blank pages where blood is white & death is near
& you would melt the metal of that moment's quarrel
& summon the colours of possibility to appear

to take the roaring from the sky & oil from the barrel
& shed the light of plenty that only Summer can
that pibrochd which feeds the inaccessible

peaks of aspiration & the straths of our shame
oh, early Summer, put the woman back into the man

make me your messenger & your skaldic tongue
season of laughter & light & love
when youth is broadened & the old grow young

take these sunlit thoughts & throw them above
the cacophony of the pitiless market
& let them sing so that their blood can move

that necessary mountain of passion & thought
& like the breather corn growing in a Caithness field
it roots in the stars to earth & not

food for only a few so the dead can wield
a steel blanket around the earth
& shut out the light & imprison the yield

of the labours of the Sun – ah, my firth
is the world a sea-bed to the salt-rose of our worth?

The View from Ben Dorrery

It is unable the rain to matter
nor the air to shake its hair
the land seeks solace from the shore
to feel the shapes no longer there
these absences which sing out from the sea
lie naked & invisible from Morven to Dunnet Head
remembered in forgetting how to be
so the living are connected to the dead

emptiness like a grey crayon colours the sky
& buries it at the source of Thurso river
& the brown reactionary language of the hills
gives our thwarted plateau its southern shoulder
dropped in indifference to the passer-by
that ultimate salute of an indifferent history

if the wind through the birch trees
is the language of the missing
then peat is their grammar
captured & transformed
a natural forest into mud's cousin
thick & moist, heady
the gluttonous memory
of a transported tongue
with these the winters court the summers
from loch to bog to clachan
in the soft black calendar of witness
to go beneath to the root, to the stone
to this the rain will testify
like a hand painted on a wall
spread out & stencilled in time
with the powdered magic of blood
a 'naive & brutal freedom'
all is missing
even as it folds back on itself
into the feminine past
still missing

Young Rowan

The summer's failure rose above the sodden county
until its very art became invisible
below the grey listless clouds
the black-haired woman sleeps
by a stocky wall a young rowan shivers
in the dying promise of the wind

the de-commissioning buildings come together
in the conversation of a camp
& like that enforced eloquence
will leave no lasting imprint
on the carefully scarred map of this voyage
charted by CCTV cameras & industrial gloves

from their urban bothy they looked across
the unbuilt ground to the maternity hospital
in which no longer anyone is born
Accident & Emergency too has gone
soon fog will roll in from the firth
covering Olrig Hill in a hazy skin

that ungiving summer was when the Free Kirk split apart
one time too many & this time for money
Another squall argues in from the west
& the young rowan now is bending
bowing seawards in forced supplication
Here on the cliff's edge the town is hermetically sealed

around the place the lucky & the afflicted
build dubious mansions in which to dress
the excellence of their absurdity in the necessary material
it takes to need a double garage
looking ever inwards through soundproof windows
the Atlantic drums out an architecture of sea anchors

to the very ones who will never hear that rhythm
for as the rain abates it is the dog walkers
who will inherit the tarmac & the neon light
a blue van is parked by a brown wooden shed
inside the deal is done
afterwards the mobile phones are switched on again

Seeking Angels

The summer footballers' whistles sing
across the atomic town
Mrs Cowie measures the rainfall
in disappearing centimetres
& behind the willow tree the midnight moth
flutters silent & white
unaware of time & title
from this the headland is but a mythology away

they climbed a hillag, looked back
the peat banks spread out
like brown green terraces
humanity had cut a cart track to somewhere

from her work she looked up
& saw them
beside her a man with a tusker
carried on
the two boys scuttled back & forth
scaling
above them
the sky was an ochre revolution
the dubh lochs held the sky
in an anchorage of wool

there is a cairn upon the hillag
beside it she weeps
behind the intangible comfort of distance
the sun goes down
he buries his spades
under clods of turf
the family leaves
the hill is empty
except for expectation

they come off the headland
get into their metallic French guitar
of a car
& drive back through the crofts

to the nuclear town
to the rain
seeking angels
in the strange game of creosote
corner kicks
& history

Orkney Antigone

Across the firth like a summer
the fulmar which lives inside her
& dreams of clifftops & sandeels
flies through the endless air
where wings make paintings
as they beat
from the salt skin ocean tip
to the sandstone ledges
a community of the necessary ingredients
supplying landscape, sea, clouds
with their measured beauty
with their imagination's flight
her eyes peat brown
with sleeping trout
the music of her hair
a calendar

The Darkening Ground

Where are the stars, The Plough
on a September Thursday at half past eight
with McDonough's play in Thurso High School
& darkness seeping over Claredon?

The river is silent in the autumn night
how quick are the rich to acquire that space
I am rendered alone in the butcher shop of lost causes
Oh, hear me, God, from thy dwelling place out at Dounreay

but know this: that the Devil has the best Geiger counters
& that Ali Moonshine will drive his JCB
deep into your sub atomic heart
where Pat Grant is a black torch usherette

welcome, my father, my holiness, my sunset
because of the ever changing nature of reality
which I know, in your book, is bad theology
look, September inks out the summer

oh, great artist
the best is growing in the darkening ground

St Andrews Night in Helmsdale

The strath is frozen like snatched love
in the back seat of a Highland bus
a purple sea, a violet expectancy
the country runs up like a wave to a pier
shows its arse & laughs
itchy from the frost
buttocks tense like rutting deer

the exploding bannock of creation
has peppered the sky with a million options
Scotia's parliament
oh, fiery monkey, time
three bottles of strong cider
& a busy all night party of one
Brahmin in the council estate

has brought the silver-hoofed horse down
to see progress as its awkward walk
with ice on its tail
& beyond that a broken harbour
& the usual brown-coloured litmus
which could be mistaken for something
in a place where no one sings
Hallelujah!

If there are saints
hidden in the mythology
let them be recycled
shredded like newspaper
or burned like car tyres
on the summit of Bheinn Bunillidh
which is hardly friendly
but St Andrew is hardly a saint
as he watches generations of mothers
washing corruption from the steps
of his cathedral

The Key

(For Angus Calder, Xmas 2003)

I was searching for an answer
& you sent me a key
literally, small & bronzy
cut into a strange version of Africa
it fell out of the envelope
like a secret
a token hidden beneath
a Mesopotamian brick
a slave cipher
bright in a mud loaf of straw
it opened up Xmas
& let in the ocean
& now a river runs
from the drawer I put it in

a hinge of liquid
a key of salt
a question a lion asks
of the night

Pink Moon over Yarrows

Your face washed in the blood of the sun
wiped pink by the red handkerchief
of the woman who guards the burial mounds
she has bidden us all here: now you are our banner

she sits by the Loch of Yarrows
knitting the music of water from twigs
all these stones she has summoned
down from heaven into the cairns of sleep
watching the sky cut footprints
from those who lived in & under her handiwork
she has made her three sisters
from pillars of stone
has stuck her flint knife
into their flagstone shoulders
sewn footprints to their skirts
so all will follow them
past honey, barley, deer
into the casket of the earth

pink moon
the blood of the sun flows from their shoulders
all the people gathered under your banner
are similarly cut & the stones fall like rain
around the bowl of Yarrows
the woman spreads her handkerchief
across the sloping sides of the heather hills
catches them & rebuilds her sisters
again & again for six thousand years
sharpening her flint knife by the side of the loch
to cut a thread of music
& sew once more the makers of fields
to the meaning of stones, of light
& the renewable resource of blood

The Silver Road

(For the Palestinian Dead)

The night peels itself like a fruit
& in his father's arms
the young boy bleeds
& waits for freedom to take root

in the earth-baked acres
which surrounded the sun-soaked town
at the end of the silver road
where the night is blood on the words

of the soldier's panic so they take him away
but not far enough
because the road is too long
& it's the end of the day

& the night is a stretcher
where he lies stiff by his father's side

For a Rousay Mare

I lay down in the long soft grass
by a still & gentle harbour
looking on islands & ship-tight firths
where sky & land became a telescope
for a thousand unbroken years
where a dance band plays in an island hall
& the people reel from year to year
& drink their tea & rum & laugh
as if they remember Troy
the birds are in the song-lit sky
the beetles in the welcoming ground
the terns on the holm are weaving
a pattern from seaweed & stars
& I will sleep like Aengus tonight

with my pockets full of dreams

Homer's Seal

A young seal suns himself off Thurso beach
in the September sun-blue Autumn
he dreams about his past
as overhead the seagulls scream

he remembers when the town
was a series of sand dunes
& he used to lie there in his hundreds
before human-kind had made a home

this far north
before the snow
in the days
of the world's morning

when flotillas of whales
would lie off Holborn Head
& between Dwarick & Dunnet
herring boiled the sea

the young seal remembers this
with his tail arched up like a fan
& the gentle waves washing him
as the sea does for those she loves

he sees a man with a notebook & pen
when he first swam into the bay
it was a grey ambergris of wind & rain
now he is surrounded by Homer's Aegean

he is as black
as ebony
perfect in the power
of dream's transformation

The Memory of Oysters

Beyond the tide line, at the end of dream
where the black & white somnambulists dance
wearing these cliffs like scarves & gloves
petitioning us with our silence
to abandon all our stunted steeples
& our loves
as a boy throws photographs onto a fire
all those burning faces
with their fingerprints of a tractor tyre
he craves his freedom as the tide goes out
& feigns a fond affection for his father's clout
in that broad area of mirror
where the sea has surrendered
until her sister the moon
encourages her to be the sucking counter
in the sleepless pas-de-bas of aspiration
of the shameless naming of your name
& you script it then into the wet sand
your signature to the world
ah sleep, have pity on the child

Andromeda

The beginning of December is as still as a nut
as the evening pours itself into the sea
between the winking automatic eyes
of Dunnet & Holborn Head
a ship slices across Thurso Bay
hungry for Scrabster pier
& the rum-soaked counter of Popeye's Bar

the land is like an eyelid
that is closing on the day
the neon necklace of Scrabster agrees
as lorries pass crammed full of Xmas trees
the thinning of all our Xmases to come

the darkening sky is as large as the inside of my head
& as tiny as the perimeters of that
& there's nothing contained that hasn't
passed this way before
as four o clock will bring me to my knees
for this could be the Antilles
or this could be the Aegean
where Hector & Achilles play
but the wind that is gathering
around this singularity of north
brushes those coloured chalk marks from the page
it will take you with it when it goes

Visions in the Dark

Out there is Sutherland
& over its black shoulder
is Caithness
keeking like a ghost

She strokes his head
as erotic as adding
I do not know their destination
these train bound strangers

no one invites the next minute of oxygen
it arrives like a lung
involved & vital
& everything has changed

2
No one knew how my great grandfather made his money
but like white teeth rumour does not travel

Scrabster harbour is not a denture set
& Ormlie Lodge no orthodontist's cap

& yet his mason's image persists
with my great grandmother sitting in the garden

beside a beehive & a dead ringer for Queen Victoria
her bun the black absolute arithmetic of death

such was hair & morality in the late nineteenth century
& as angry as a swarm of bailiffs life went on

3
Geordie Crowden waddles towards his creels
& the existential Presbyterian revolution

like a fat penguin on roller skates
the pier jutting out into the sea like a stone pulpit

& his eyes like two corrugated tin roof sheets
& the wet piss stain of a careless insurrection

spreading across his gowl like a tide
as he turns the key in the bothy door

which opens onto a Sunday of beaches, fields & cliffs
& the memory of a mason who bred a farmer
                                        who bred a crofter

4

Across the bay, cupped like petals
in the hand of a new dead Egyptian
words drift like smoke
from the distant Winter bonfires

flickering over Dunnet Bay like iced butterflies
coated in peat
they follow no course
& obey no laws other than that of essence

My great grandmother shook her head
because some bee had annoyed her
& two strathsfull of people
& a fleet of transport boats

fell out of her harvest-stacked hair

5

The train moves on, ploughing into the northern night
as if furrowing a field of hours to make ready for memory

the people are stilled, like seeds in a lofted sack
tied at the neck by the umbilical cord of railtrack & boredom

My father said you looked at this Caithness Victoria
& wet your breeks if like a bee you gave offence

so now the gradual assimilation of ages has begun
& years gather in hundreds like sheaves of winter barley

you cannot count back in Caithness
you cannot count forward in Sutherland

for the ghosts are still keeking
urging everything onwards

to anchor on the god-rocks
of churchyards, bones, masons, beehives

The King of the Herring

I should be dancing
I dream of flying
through the spicy
itchy air of medieval bird wings
& I would love to stick
the stars upon the firmament
which is everlasting
as Blue-tack
but I am busy here as a refugee
down on the ground
while wars are raging
in heaven
I search in the sea-loch
for the king of the herring

Claredon

With effortless urgency
the morning breaks
pouring light over the edge of Caithness
a painter preparing to paint

the red cloth of the day's beginning
is cut by the blade of the sun
& the sky unfolds
the sharpened images

carefully like cutlery
touched once
then melted down
for another pigment

the world is impatient with itself
& the dawn cannot wait to be alone
such slow time is too swift
the birds encircle the song

as if in such gathering
they are returning
like Dorrud after he saw
the twelve Valkyrie over Claredon

2

Weaving, weft & warp
load your bullets
on your tongue
this message is a shirt

wearing the red dawn & four names
was Dorrud really looking in a window
is the sky always an entrance
so vast, like an armoury?

it will not rain
blood – yet
clouds of ocean
pass through the heddles

as ships do between headlands
hours pull the web tight
colour up the pattern
with aching crimson

relieving itself
a slow avalanche
of the common phenomenon
the pages of this book are peeled like rain

3

The lucky dawn is doomed
they rode into the story
like disciples yet they needed no saint
only the touch of intestines

& skulls, their favourite tapestry
patched upon the conscience
like a name
you will whisper it to the South

& then to the North
& then rip its fragment
a patch of identity
into ribbons of meaning

then you go
the weave a pink vapour
the cutting schedule
has come to this

on some other islands
they may see the same
wish it well on them
how everything opens

4

The orchestra of the Sun is up
waking into a symphony
across the flat fields
the winter green is pulsing

into brown, come thin bird
into this music of agriculture
& knitting, let the yellow light
sew your wings to purpose

& what itchy music there is
let history find it
your wings are perfect crayons
hear the arrogant insistence of endings

between horizon & grace
the dazzling god
of winter, soar & hover
because the air is kind to you

do not suppose that desolation is here
do not accept our gentle irrelevant wars
fly like this mustard light
into the singing moment

5

Behind the crow's cry is white silence
beak to beak with the immediacy
of how that never ends
& goes behind Claredon Hill

six sides to every face of the story
& two faces to every side
with the definite knowledge
that clouds are still up there

on their silver strings
a blue weave
now the sky is haemorrhaging light
so low it shines beneath the feet

so behold, pilgrim, the impossibility of reason
here on this grey coast
where angels shrug in queues
to behold

the green sails
fluttering through a dream
out west
beyond The Hebrides

In Memoriam Jimmy Pandora

A Poem for Five Voices

(The numbering relates to the voice speaking)

1

We are the dome dwellers
we live in the side of the hill
we wear reinforced goldfish bowls
around our heads

We are the dream de-constructors
we will pull your rainbows down
in the north light
& imagine some tragedy

will unfold if we do not participate
with our forecasts & our demographics
our stick-on economics

2

With all this they will bury Jimmy Pandora
who lived all his life at The Niss
crafting his permitted acres
until they ground him down

with design & isolation
pouring concrete over his parks
his neep drills like cemetery rows

3

In the autumn of our industry
we are startled by the night
the storm has come too early
for the lamps to be lit

In the deserts the supermarkets will flower
emptying boxes so we can enjoy the sand
I salute you in your endeavour
I would never dream to criticise

such a proud & worthy enterprise
siphoning off the clouds from the sky
as we expire

4

Jimmy Pandora, the sea is blue grey today
as it was when Cormack crossed the strand into this music
& set his sandalled foot
on island, headland, fireplace

In a cornered kist there lies
a photograph from years ago
your fields are full of hay & potatoes
& the void of bungalows has not yet come

we are alone
we were young
we were all together

5

In the clay above the flagstone beds
you sleep beneath Barrock Hill
while one thousand years stood still
all around you

& memories will not come with the crying & the cars
but will lie with the rusting implements
abandoned on the cliff tops
like history's oxidizing moustache

& you may well ask
what else is there for them to do
now that the ground is parched?

4

They will carry you past the croft house museum
down the narrow road
to the stone ship of the kirk
with its Norwegian wash blue walls

& varnished pine carvings rune-rolling
like a calligraphic wave from pew to pew
& they will celebrate you between the psalms
find salvation in the organ music

wafting across the bay like acoustic rum
& they will sing
as though they would rather be at sea

1
For we are the domed people
we signed the sheets for silence
& tattooed our slogans on the wind
we lament the passing of the binder

while gladly waving in the combine harvester
so we should not be surprised
when we look out of their eyes
& see ourselves looking in

2
They wrap harmony in a membrane
build camps to house the moon
they will chisel marble harbours
in the shifting tidal firth

they will construct bridges across the midnight
& car parks to accommodate the Sun
duly elected to damnation we follow on

1
We wear our reinforced goldfish bowls
with acquired harvest refugee pride
exiled within our miles

4
See, Jimmy Pandora
they are driving around & around
the dream of sheaf & creel
who will go down into the receptive ground

clean of years, of masks
knowing that the Earth is a photograph
of itself taken by one who patrols
on the far side of the trout-itchy loch

they file past you a century long
from war to war their meanings stick
& now that the fire-curtain we call peace is lowered
your closed crofter's eyes are all

the applause this play of years deserves
you go now & join a list of names
scratched on stone
anchoring us all to the particles of change

3

Salmon nets drying like salt-soaked trampolines
three fields from your sheep-dipper
my brother & I as thin as hares
would bounce above the dunes

& below the turning tide-line
with the mid-summer hay bales
the shock absorbers for the approaching drum-sound
from Dwarick Head to Dunnet

a shawl wrapped around the shoulders
of a sleeping girl
a quilt of purpose beside a broad bay

5

Sutherlands, Calders, Oags
moved on patronymics of a century's
resolution landed here in this cupped palm
ploughed furrows the markings of an individual hand

the wet peat colour of the matrilineal soil
no earth-ghosts or sea-shapes there
but the residual evidence of a social song
which marries its melody to the theory of science

for no energy is destroyed here
on shoreline or in turr-wake
it is only transferred as if in a boat
from one side of the firth to the other

& here we stop
to cross again
in the ship from dark to light

1

So now beyond the music of the north
we dome-dwellers are secure
in our ferried-in desert
particle by particle we create

a long white dune of noise
which will fill our heads
with static & no protection
will be of use to us

We will have emptied the hill
& wrapped ourselves in graphs
distant at the centre of the world

3

Go now, Jimmy Pandora

An Empty Spring

(after Pablo Neruda)

You will ask: where are the shochads?
 I will point out to you the empty fields
& the iron sound of an empty Spring

You will say: these days are longer
I will say that they are too long
& that silence is stone sugar

You will point to the young stars
I will cover my eyes from the flames
as the ancient plague virus spreads

as the carcass pyres burn a funeral of cattle
as they dig a hungry trench
as animals pour into a system of failure

I will ask: where are the crocuses?
You will point to the paintings of Matisse
& the grey ship of a cloud

I will say the smoke & smell are choking
you will say this is the new skyscape
to cover up the closed ground

I will point to you & you will point to me
we will be like a wind-vane
pushed into the prevailing sorrow of detergent

as the counting of heads goes on
as the steading gate is shut
as our eyes melt into tractor tyres

of an empty Spring

Hill Burning

They are burning the hill
its brown hair combed
with the orange teeth of flames
brown to black in smoky transformation
the mattress of heather
burnt back to a hard board
the tapestry of the hillside
turned into a charcoal slate
once the itchy fires have done with it

this is the regeneration of Spring
when the icy spider of Winter
has her cobwebs cleared
when the old grey growth
must make way for the new green promise
that lies beneath the ground
enticed out by heat & space
this is the hill putting on its new coat
which will change from bare peat to purple

into this she stepped older now
but still intent on performing the ritual
the morning was a blue scarf
upon the head of a young girl
she did not notice the flames kiss her skirt
nor see the smoke which embraced her
she lay beside the burn for four hours
before anyone found her

still smiling

Let Us Compare Ravings

Bearing in mind that Scotland is fascinated by dualities
doubles, doppelgangers, opposites, twins
the yin & the yang of high & low
ripping apart ambivalences like two fish
swimming in the opposite direction
the far side of the universe
the top & roost on the tree of life
& death the wrong side of the causeway
where two tides meet, night & day
forever old & young are men & women
laughing sad tears into the wet sand
on the dry land centred at the middle
of the edge I turn to you & ask you this

Post Democracy 2001

I go & vote with a red nose
in a green coriander Summer
of threatening buildings
& trapped butterflies
caught between the window
& the colour of rain
longing to dance
beside Magnus & the other dubious ones
in a garden of pins
chanting plainsong apologies
for inappropriate religions
of dressed sandstone & paschal candles
putting black blood
up on the cross, again

I have known the inexorable sadness of pencils
                                    – Theodore Roethke 1908–63

Orkney Skald
(For Alistair Peebles)

Tales of fishing & poetry
in the harbour
where Summer can be hailstones
& the black clouds of a northern June
& I think
Beethoven used to break the instruments
he laid his hands upon
we will renew
what we must renew
a hawk's perch of gold & fire
on the wind's roof
as easily as the earth sprung out of the sea
skalds make the sky
spring bright across Orkney

Scotscalder
(For David Morrison)

A skein of geese in a grey Caithness sky
points me across the flat lands
to the mountains in the south

Red deer hinds run through the heather
with itchy nostrils like a Friday night
& back in the small Viking town

Robbie downs his dram
spinning with shadows & histories
& the occasional light

I hold them in the cup of my hand
like a hill loch hosting dragonflies
this is our land

& betrayal is unforgivable
the towers give them away
as Autumn browns the hill

As easy as walking along a road
the news came of the impending end
so cheery were the newsreaders

you couldn't help but share
in their glad gibberish
of this & that

& three thousand now are dead
a shadow crosses the road
& everything we know is wrong

Events, like tides, are predictable
& yet like an incredible dawn
they amaze us with their inevitable beauty

we have been ground down
& now we are smooth to horror
& the urgent blackness of our time

what we have done is done
& like Homer's evocations
cannot be undone

& we wait for night
a solitary people
on the edge of red sandstone cliffs

so quiet is tragedy & full our span
it is as though we cannot recognise our own names
& have become chiselled from crazy luck

we expect the stars to explain themselves
while we have forgotten
how to listen to music

this cannot last
someone else's song is being played
no-one is immune

nothing rises in the wrong place
except hell
& the American flag

World Trade

Two dragonflies landed
on two standing stones
which stood
beside a river
& were part of an ancient city

The dragonflies died
& the stones crumbled
the river turned red
& the city froze
in the ruins

Progress

The first steps of the spacewalk
were fashioned in Dachau

the sun shines upon Thurso
it is duly monitored

October Moon

The grass is the colour of rain
in this Autumn of low horizons
late harvests
& sodden barley

The sky holds the darkness
of your hair
as the ditches drink
doubt, danger & corruption

The busy cliffs of the flagstone lap
rejoice shaking their castanets
of fossil slate & ancient light
silver as a Spanish plate

in a stone field
The stars are torch-cut holes
pulling the sea through the tired
consequences of power

walking away across distant mountains
easy in words & the end of meaning
the everyday war of shoreline
& the hidden silhouette of the sliding moon

in this darkening, ever darkening October
how delicate is this art
this paper, this ink
unsuccessful against the coming screens

of night & the moon in your face
the reluctant signature of recognition
words graze by meaning's roadside
& grow nervous in the headlights' glare

all is passing, trees bend in the wind
the month is crouching
in the fields wet unwelcoming corner
& your eyes shine cobalt through the silence

of engines, whips & the mechanics
of make believe
we live without honour
through days of sunless expectancy

this series of flowerless ideas
as The Plough hangs like a collar
in the blue neep-tide magnet
in a season of aching & nouns

they lie wasted like small mussel shells
abandoned within their own iodine
or like tiny pink scallops
whose death was their infancies' end

all are littered, incomplete & terrible
in their stunting possibility
with their sheer number no compensation
for the blind beauty of their creation

you will walk along this surf-kissed beach
the October moon in the Orkney of your hair
& you will forgive the rain
the reminder it sends to the thirsty ditches

The Republic Begins

She took her hat off
& lay down at the beginning
of the century's dance
waved goodbye with her bones
& hung her hat on a passing mediocrity
& ministers & highland games organisers
praised her for being sober
(when she never was)
& magazine editors noticed
that she talked to everyone
(when she only ever talked to herself)
they are burying the monkey
as the share price falls
here in the broad acres of heaven

Design for a Machine
to Make Things Go Slower

Would it be that your heart
has to be hurt like the firth
pumping the vast oceans
between these high cliffs

& the island & the croft coast
of nineteen fifty six?

I would dare you to imagine
love like this
how it picks us up
awkward like two reluctant seas

& transports us like a shoal of mackerel
from one salt breeding ground to the next
interrupting, like the moon,
our feeding frenzy

A Kyle on the North Coast of Sutherland
(After a photograph)

It's Summer, a woman & a man
sit on a wall in front of a
silver beach & blue sea
she is sixty, maybe younger
he is nineteen, maybe older
there is a small dog, a Jack Russell
it is Summer, it looks like
Bettyhill, the woman seems to be
waiting, the man has
his left hand to his neck
& a pint, three-quarters-drunk
in his right hand & for some reason
everything has Sunday written on it
the dry-stane wall behind them
is a perfect liquid skin & a
hidden sign asks & hopes that
everybody does thirty, some whins
grow, sheep graze, it is not
an unusual picture except
that the women would duly kill
herself, the dog would die of cancer
& the son would ruin everything he touched
the sky is thin blue like calor gas
there is the suggestion of grey mountains
somewhere far away & it can be said
that if it were not for the exactness of this photo
it would be about anybody anywhere
anyway, it's Summer.

A Lifejacket for Shelley

Frightened by the volcano we think of something big
while settling for what we have
which is nothing & we spin a tune
& we smile a lot while being grave

I'm swallowing lava, I'm going back to the top
& looking down, all this sorrow
is queuing to be cleansed
I'm clutching at yesterday, groping for tomorrow

because it looks like something I should know
tell me all about it, Percy
when you took your last drink
did you die more gloomy than merry

did you die with your hands in your pockets
did your leather boots float past
did the fish nibble at your eye sockets
tell me, how long did your death last

do you know the volcano of which I speak
it is rumbling in the place from which I come
I see your spittle hiss off a rock
I won't settle for what I've got, my name

is on this life jacket which I hold
I'm going to throw it to you, Shelley
I won't let you die, no no
there's a new volcano in my belly

it's your dreams, it's your burning voice
let us conspire to boil the sea
let the regulators of boredom drown
this life jacket will set you free

we can dance to the evaporation of apathy
that in the first place got you wet
we can ski on the hot ideas
no one has ever had as yet

our coastland is falling apart, the rocks
crash into the sea
with hapless enthusiasm, hold on
to that life jacket, Shelley, & be

a small god in a sinking world
the water aerated to the point of death
nothing floating because of the gas
seeping out from the formation of wealth

a natural thing turned unnaturally fatal
swallowing us up in its hungry mouth
& we host chat shows & we go down
our fingers pointing north & south

divided like a set of flare-off booms
or as the hinge is from the latch
we see a grey storm coming in
here's a life jacket for you, Shelley, catch

hold it firm & wear it well
keep it on at all times
I hear a grey man ring a grey bell
listen to its grey midnight chimes

& with that tolling in our ears we must surely
emerge from the bubbling water
buoyant at last in some kind of entente
the mother, the father, the son & the daughter

on a life-raft of interwoven tongues
the sea is blood, the sea is fire
the sea is the world's sweating skin
from this we shall inspire

the moon to bestill the tides
in the jasmine ocean of our desire
come now to our essential rock
come now night, stars & fire

in this thick blue light our expectations
are the sea horses rolling before the beach
our ears & tongue define the nations
the geography of mind has left out of reach

searching for these strange small gods with broken wings
who breathe upon us to make the stones float
& I will fuel my volcano because it is there
& point with glee to all the things it is not

& there beneath the salmon pool of your eye
swim Bo Derg, Aengus & Mannan
with Bhrigid somewhere not far behind
& us stuck like flies to the trap of Canaan

Lu, Dagda, turning our bodies to the very vapour
we chase in our loud dreams
here all things must stir
& from dull mud make art that gleams

but will not dazzle eye or mind
but shine like stars in the sky overhead
& trigger that alchemical thing
which make the living dance with the dead

which makes the birds & the fishes sing
I beg you, Shelley, do not be late
I hear the bells of the Atlantic ring
out beyond the current of love & hate

it pulls the moon to us instead of us to it
my prayers are old oars on a new boat
this is the perfect life jacket, poet
wear it on your words, your tongue, your throat

you will speak oceans, seas, lochs
your poems are like salmon in a swollen river
struggling against the world to be reborn
into a time that is both a blink & forever

& below all this these hapless ones
stand like cattle in a storm
rumps to the wind in thunder & fear
their blood running cold as yours runs warm

as we hear the whispered evocations of Etain
the goddess of life jackets & Gaelic love
who satisfies all primitive need
to have our heaven below & our hell above

so we swim through the circles of Lir
from outer infinity to the middle ring
& then to the next of the inner waters
which lead to the inner world everlasting

so beware, Bysshe, it's some vest that you wear
a brand new god you should have known before
& if it's any consolation
I believe in neither ship nor shore

singing sorrow, singing "Hey, Mr Death
what have you got to say to me?"
I wondered where my voice had gone
I saw its bow cut across the sea

& then I saw the face of Death
her voice I knew quite well
over centuries it's made the poets sweat
lent a bony hand to ring that bell

she slurred to me "Come in here, son
ah hev a place for ye"
& she held out her tinker's hand
such a gamely dame was she

she took me to where you're biding, Shelley
in the fousty scullery of shelves & books
hold on, for the small gods' sake, hold on
freedom is in the crannies & nooks

what rescue is complete without a tragedy
here is mine, they park their bayonets
at the bottom of the stairs
we do not own, we have seasonal lets

if you were to be washed ashore, Shelley
it would be here on Dunnet Beach
beside the parazone bottles & the plenty
a set of perfections too out of reach

just like this life jacket I throw to you
it is far too little far too late
we move onward & we move through
the broken silence to the loud checkmate

is this just hopeless Gallaidh speculation
or do small gods & life jackets really matter
have we nailed our tongue to the Sitka spruce
& tuned our senses to London patter

small groups gather in the dark
some change, some get broken
but at last the substance from the husk
pours through & the green god of truth, she is spoken

Corncrake

From the wet corner of a field at the end of June
I would hear your rattle twist calling out
through the green hay crop to your rival
or your mate, unseen, always unseen
although the once I did see you I laughed
at your resemblance to my mother's scrubbing brush
sweet ugly bird, are you thirsty, corncrake
since you have flown over the Sahara Desert
to get here, to this Caithness croft park
how welcome you are, how annoying
"If ah see they hoors, ah'll shot thum," my father
blared, semmit-clad in the simmer dim at 3 am
but what care you or I for that, bird & boy
each in their wet corner, awake & noisey

Caithness

If I could run headless through the barley fields
I would swim the green tide of land
to Watten, say, or maybe Bower
in the flat converted boglands
where our generations found their form

I would run headless then from steading
to steading, from barn to barn
starbright in the stables & milking sheds
my headless head full of the smells of growth
& silage, ah sweet temptress life

you have strewn the stone anvils
of our northern tapestry with many gods
on our tongues sit Thor & Odin
behind our eyes bleed Christ & Columba
not often as the planet spins

will the darkness glitter like this

Norman MacLeod

What, in that sea marble head
turned from Stoer to Nova Scotia
from Cape Breton to Adelaide
from Melbourne to new Zealand

I am close to the hot blood, I am close
to the goram water & the hill
the roads that beat to Aberdeen
to Edinburgh & to Wick, how far

is the mind out ahead to follow
our calling, or is it a thin fool
on a green rock who instructs the bowing
of heads, unknown to himself the big man

unshed the sun & was happier in the desert
where some bandits found him
& gave him a horse, heaven
again, what journeys do we lend ourselves

to fill our tents & down our drams
we will construct our icons & wear
our mythology like heads in fishbowls
a Yuri Gargarin psychology where

the ear-snippers brand our clipped theology
onto the giant fears of a cast-adrift
population who find the dream shagged
like Muslim women in a Serbian pillow war

how happy I am to be here, I hear me
or someone busily distancing ourselves
from the very concept, now the sea
opens up & I am but an Egyptian wheel

some aqua-archaeologist has found while looking
for the golden breast plate of the Pharaoh's general
I feel neglected, but this is what
it's like close to the goram water

it is time, it is time, it is time for such journeys
from skull-side to skull-side, Norman
I am the holder of what you can never own
the rented icons & mythologies not found on maps

Estonia
(In Memoriam Jessie Kesson)

The day after you died, Jessie
nine hundred went to the bottom of the Baltic
& yet I grieve more for you
somehow your going is more tragic

Elgin for us northerners was always caeteran country
& I suppose for both our borders
we met & left the idea of anything
any town or place, like lovers

whose noses sniff the wind, always onward
& beyond that word, that clutch
of representational hee-haw
folk like us would never learn to love much

on that long road to the out out
of the story's beat & our people's face
in the middle of it alive in the radiant joy
of yes yes, that favourite word of our race

who shipped it over that same Baltic water
on our way to explore the Volga
ach, Jessie, ye willna be crackin wi me
nae mair: hey, quine, I'll be seein ya

Robert Lowell in Orkney

With your bi-annual collapses behind you
& your death in the back seat
of a New York taxi some six years ahead
you landed in Orkney & asked
around the Post Office & the shops of Stromness
"Where are the Spences, where are the Traills?
I am Robert Traill Spence Lowell"
& the folk of Stromness
were their usual polite selves
"Do you know them?"
"Aye"! they replied, nothing more
but in their blood sang the old song
"Traills up the toon
Traills doon the toon
Traills in the middle
Deil'll tak the Traills guts
for strings tae his fiddle"
& Sir Patrick on the high tide of his dream
so what is life but vague aspiration
or a set of scratchings on a stone?

nothing is right
the dried ling swing
like salted bats & the air
a lungful of Atlantic iodine
the street a dolphin's spine
that was Stromness that Summer

& you, Lowell, just another rich Yank
tourist back in the old world
to make your generational needs new
Orkney, however, soaks up the streams
of expectation like a hungry estuary

there are no rivers here, Robert Lowell
only beaches & the ache of a sea sad mile

we are not near the ocean
we are part of the ocean

The Rain Box

May is ending badly & this brown mud
into which my blood is turning
stews in front of box-size mythologies
which trample my nativeness as surely as a laird

I can thole no more rain & the pale Sun
seems to me a cut-price thing
wet smoke & grass like a drowned skirt
welcome Summer, Scotland is waiting

her hunker'd wisdom is a poor stool
in a church of rain clouds
yet the thing has more wings than a midgy swarm
more direction than a herring shoal

so why do I hear the dull thump of distant guns
like Gruach fearing for her sons?

Moon, Strath, Cliff

The moon is sailing
through the trees
small fire, big fire
the blood of the day
is on my tongue
the bats are happy
in the branches
I stare & stare
like time has been undone
where is the Summer that
I may walk upon the moon?
this silver obsession will
take me to the coastland
where the sea is green

& all that has been is done
there are rivers here
& fields with yellow hair
& crops will grow bright goram
I've sworn my oaths
upon these shattered shorelines
I put my trust in
the moon's grey chartings
& in the sheer cliffs
which the same moon turns
to purple but tonight
this inland strath rings
to the igneous flow
of the world's vibrant heart

Jigsaw Boy

The night after Kennedy was assassinated
we all hid under our beds
because we believed
the Russians would bomb us

I dreamed of fighter bombers
& the Confederate soldiers
you got from the back
of a Bazooka Bar

I played with all of them
on the warehouse socialism
of our front room floor
my eye to the always sea

but I was like a dropped jigsaw
some sky & some land
chasing over the smooth linoleum
an Inuit after a seal

The Coast of Widows

A broken necklace of crofts
strewn across the sandstone floor
of the north Caithness coast
these sea-beat parishes where the fields
are sea-tang & the hay has herring-dream
in root & stalk
this is where Scotland stops & starts
here faces turn to check the Pentland Firth's
anxious coupling of North Sea
to Atlantic Ocean
the incessant urgency of tide upon tide
& these same faces when the night
opens her black windows to them
look up to see the infinite cod roe

of the stars above

The Demand

As glad as a knife I cut my thigh
& hand you the slice
won't you taste it now?
it would be so revealing
I can give you more than that
I could give you arms & legs
& every other bit that you want
will you consume them soon?
the blade is still sharp you know
I take great care in its keening
you told me you were hungry once
I remember it well
I remember everything that you said
I understood the demand in your eyes

The Last of the Brambles

Purple noses in a hedge of government
the rain comes in October
through the flat feet of our administration
somewhere there is sunlight

I push my head into your bushes & bleed
perfect, the small agonies of truth
pour off like flies from a bramble
your claret home should be called democracy

but I am too late, you are saying
with love or some other Tory vote
the best thing I can do is leave
you to the elements of hope that

you ferment with the angry gods
of equality who wrestle inside my head
welcome bramble, this rough wine of Scotland

In Thurso One Night

They slip under the eiderdowns of their bodies
the young boys in the bar
resisting their fears & talking about Rangers

when they could be blessed by the soft salt dew
I feel in my hair
this morning as I walked out

to the firth, "Be strong & then be gentle"
I wanted to cry out to them
"Like those warriors when your country

was young, men who drew their women
to them as lovingly as sheaves of corn
& only put steel through hatred

don't waste your hearts on the tired
organisations of boredom"
That I didn't is part of my general failure

then the night shut like a windblown door
& Thurso seemed
to slide beneath the waves

a Caithness Atlantis
where love comes
from stones

Otters

A head appears in the rivermouth
like a small black whiskered stone
then another, reclining
with the ease of music
they chew the heads off fish

when they're done they're almost out to sea
with the practised nonchalance of Spring rain
they dive beneath the surface
& swim up the river again
are we like the otters

do we drift
& do we swim back?

Blackbird

If I were a blackbird
I would fly to your house
& nest on the roof
so that I could sing
to you each morning
of how once the world was young
& full of song
& you would hear me singing
& you would sight yourself
& the world of song
would surround you
& gently fill you up
with a green surge of longing

Cormorant

The waves are the salty eyelids of the moon
Hoy the north's eyebrow
a cormorant squats on the pier end
as black as exodus
the yellow of its throat
has swallowed testaments of fish
it shakes its head
at the ridiculousness of time
the Sun catches Dunnet Head
in a tapestry of red light
the cormorant takes flight
filling its darkness
with the green of the sea
as if nothing were pursuing it

save for the moon & the stars & Orkney

In the Pictish Navy

They saw our sails
cow lungs across the Moray Firth
pitch in our gantries
oak beneath our brogued feet

we had arrows at the ready
if we got close enough
dead Romans
like still dolphins

by the many hundred
that was our bardic dream
an old keel across Europe
three hundred ships ago

Tacitus turned to Caesar & said
"The stars are out tonight"
so they scuttled off south
to rewrite our history

Gartymore

*In memory of the Highland Land League's
inaugural meeting, 1881*

The Sunday bells of Helmsdale
drift over the April rain
chimney smoke hangs in blue columns
above the slate roofs of the village
& the harbour fingers into the sea
the hold this place has on the world
as I walk to Gartymore
through daffodils & lamb-bleat
through the Strath of Spring
the strath of resistance & fight back
Bannerman, Macleod, Watson, Fraser
a four-fold foundation for freedom
from Sellar, Young, Loch, Gordon
I climb the hill & splice the rain

Beach Anglers

It is as if they are trying to land the sea
a thinning rank of them
huddled in three two one's
plastic bucket of bait at hand
like squat thermos or valves
the bay is a grey reluctant song
they write their line music for
some yards offshore a disinterest of seagulls
bob lazily on the salt shimmer
we call the Pentland Firth

the fishermen stand waiting
for a surrender of fish
or for a revelation
& in this the sea & sky are one
they have joined gently to disappear
the horizon in an opaque crucifixion
the fishermen notice none of this
& concentrate on fish
with a collective of bait & children
playing in the sand behind them

a woman takes a photograph
as if Holborn Head might
take up its sandstone bed
& walk to become a new Atlantis
somewhere out in the deep ocean
where we can all be swallowed like a hook
& where the only miracle
is the everlasting swapping of tides
& the daily grinding of our dreams
upon the firth bed of our lives

They Are Throwing Stones at the Cows

It's cold this Summer, the angle of the coast
is hanging sharper, all the rest of the world
is a steel wave somewhere precisely
where we left it, behind the stone pile
of pronouns we use to give each other names

I look over to the far corner of the park
a young calf is cowering
its birth lies steaming some yards away
the Spring is over, the flowers are dead
in Caithness they are throwing stones at the cows

because the road is blocked
because electricity has failed
the fiddle is back on the wall
& we have on our coast
the rest of the night

Aubergines After Rain
(For Askell Masson)

There was a bang like cannon
it blew the sky away
from bale-park to beyond
the farmland was noise
then silence
as if the sky had separated from the land
then rain
torrential
so much rain
Europe was a river
pouring down into the sea
of my birth
nothing could hold that much ocean
so pure & violent
the earth became a wave
then it stopped
a grey minute
then a wind
soft at first
from the west
then like an argument
it chased itself
from Durness to Duncansby
liberating gravity
from the byre-ends of the county
I scarpered from so much weather
like a crab on the firth-bed
of a storm
for a storm it was
like an education
so blunt & sharp
it covered up our years in its moment
then the wind died
& the sky reformed
& the land crept back within its boundaries

& a piano sounded
in my brain or some other
& our land was washed purple
like aubergines after rain
so succulent & delicate
it wore its rebirth
as a seal wears the sea
& then the morning
spread itself
across the bread slice
of Scotland's north coast
& I looked into its orange beginning
& you had gone
with the rain
& the aubergines

Warm Evening Nocturne

The poet raged for blood & white eagles
while sitting at his desk

the poet's mother's eyes were black ghosts
so he ran to the nearest war

the poet fell in love with the war
while writing poems about compassion

the poet loved the people of the war
but the people of the war hated him

the poet hated the people of his own country
the people of his own country wanted him back

to write about them

Crows on Budget Day

The crows build their nests
on budget day
while the red cliffs of Hoy shine
through the Spring's nesting promise
of ten pence on the pound

& the twigs fall down
on budget day
& the crows caw & cak
in the industry of their building
that must be built

& cigarettes & whisky
build clouds of paper
& crows shit lime
on interest rates
& savage the air with beaksful

of black crow noise
both undertaker & midwife
on budget day
to the cars of the passers by
& the flat green fields laugh

with the rookish tongues
of things that find
it difficult to matter
on budget day
two thousand years from grief's beginning

where on a tree hung another nest
& when Caesar rose up to talk
the crows still built
in a paperless mess of twigs
& blood

Turbot

You are through the house reading
there is fish everywhere
you spread your eyes like a net
across a firth of which there are thousands

all hell is breaking loose beneath
a banana skin
the river of night is dark
like the history of Rome

I met some strange angels in Melness
dark they were & well suited
some smoked cigarettes
they talked to me as if they knew me

I met them at a funeral of one they were supposed
to love – I came home, black
as though I had caught cancer
& believed in nothing

tonight the moon is a yellow duster
what is a fish?– it is
everything we know for we are all fish
drifting into the net

Monkey Ode
(A Prelude)

I'm listening to the electric monkeys
on the misty hill of Ormlie
in a cold April
before our complexion changes
& our bowels become the terrain for tanks
tonight all classical music sounds like Abba
& brown haired barmaids
become the stern Valkyrie
taking meaning to its feasting hall
after battle has consumed it
like the greatest hits
of popular democracy
pushing its shopping trolley
down the throat of reason
as if Breughal had crawled
drunk along Traill Street
& asked where Hell was
they have pointed him here
to this jukebox mound
of council housing & bad enterprise
I see him now beginning to paint
in this steam-pressed series of mouths
where we are collecting full stops
like cigarette coupons
& we can vote & vote
& blister like paint under heat
& Breughal's brush is a dancing diva
& she sings to me she sings
the days are too long
the nights are too short
anger wears a string vest
& sunbathes on Muckle Flugga
hope is dealing smack in Fraserburgh
the TV is a torn retina
& the electric monkeys

are singing Hallelujah
Hallelujah as a new chaos is born
here in this northern town
where we nail our representation down
shagging freedom behind a whin bush
oh I will not go I will not go
along with it
& the diva sings
with yellow coconuts in her hair
do the solutions
have to be cast in iron
& do elected politicians
have to turn into Agamemnon
monkey monkey monkey
we're dancing to your tune
here high on misty Ormlie
we are turning out the light

Responses to *Winter Barley*

He's Laureate of the Grey Coast, but poet and dramatist George Gunn is much more. A close focus on the native Caithness he returned to some years ago makes it both bedrock and springboard for his creative energies. Dunnet Head, its environs and other topographical features become iconic elements in the poems bringing the reader into a strong sense of familiarity with that landscape. From there the poet sends his imagination out across time and geography, to trawl in poems that glisten with a questing vitality. Incident and character are caught in the turn of a phrase. Clearance is indicted in 'The View from Ben Dorrery' where "emptiness like a grey crayon colours the sky, while 'Orkney Antigone' is one of many pure unalloyed lyrics woven through this collection.

Gunn is perpetually alert to the significance of myth and history as well as to the absurdities and tragedies our contemporary leaders inflict upon us. From that fertile patch of territory he inhabits, using metaphor as a filter, he perceives the world, in all its chaotic complexity, with a singular clarity of vision. This collection reveals a man who has a confident sense of place, and of belonging, who is yet restlessly driven to test and tease the language he uses, always concerned to make it new. From his Grey Coast, George Gunn's poetic gift sends him on a perpetual search for new horizons.

– Aonghas Macneacail

George Gunn is a poet of energy and lyricism. Fearless. *Winter Barley* reaffirms his place as the authentic voice of the North. Rooted in his landscape of calm and fury in a Caithness Atlantis "where love comes/ from stones", he rejoices in the grey argument of firth, offering a world view as rigorous as it is humane.

These extraordinary poems do not celebrate some soft rural idyll. They may be flayed with light, visually sensual – Gunn's subtle use of colour expands each poetic space – but they are above all muscular, industrial, political. Combative. Gunn writes with all the music and passion of a Neruda. Curiously, for all that his work speaks to our great late poets, MacLean, MacCaig, Crichton Smith, for all that it sings of the stretching Caithness floes, it is the Spanish poets he brings to mind in his search for the green god of truth.

For Gunn poetry is a green surge of longing, an itchy music – words pouring like light. He is aware how delicate is this art, this paper, this ink, aware that the prophet-poet is not always welcome, may be abandoned alone in the butcher's shop of lost causes. Not that this holds him back. He knows the power of dream's transformation and also the salt-rose of our worth. We *will* renew, he promises the Orkney Skald, what we *must* renew.

There are riches in every line. Gunn has both heart and sure technique. His poems, long and short, dance on the page like shot silk, like barley whiskers in northern sun. They dance and sing. In *Winter Barley*, Gunn offers us his clear and distinct music. His world. Our world. I don't know when I enjoyed a collection more.

– Anne MacLeod

George Gunn's work is as deeply informed by the landscape and history of Thurso and Caithness as George Mackay Brown by his native Stromness and Orkney, but it is not limited in any way by that. His political awareness is global in span, and human in sympathy. Caithness is a microcosm revealing the macro.

Formally, though the verse is free and the rhythms sometimes halting, Gunn's is a highly stylised poetry. It harks back to the Beats of half a century ago in its stern refusal of even the most minimal of punctuation and in employment of that most distinctive of marks from the age of the typewriter, the ampersand. There is a rich vein of imagery, of metaphors and symbols that at times suggest surrealism. It is, once the reader is familiar with it, an instantly recognisable voice.

The overriding impression is of a powerful lyrical impulse married to an equally powerful political conscience, causing the poetry to jar and shock by its sudden twisting of intent. It is not an easy 'country poetry' but echoes in its forms the sudden occurrence of industrial Dounreay on the smooth Caithness coastline, the atomic age forced upon the ageless – or the fleeting seasonal appearance of the pageant of Royalty at the Castle of Mey among the egalitarian cycle of 'common' life.

George Gunn is a mature poet at the height of his creative powers, sure of his voice and his material, a poet of conscience. His work is combative and cantankerous, opinionated and informed. At times over the past twenty-five years he has been omitted from anthologies and surveys of the contemporary poetry scene in Scotland. The publication of *Winter Barley* should make such omission impossible in future.

– Robert Alan Jamieson

Biographical Note

George Gunn was born and brought up in Dunnet, a village on the north coast of Caithness. The headlands, red sandstone cliffs and sweeping landscapes of Scotland's far north are inspiration for his poetry and form the backdrop to much of *Winter Barley*.

Since age 16 he has spent years wandering round Scotland and other parts of the world searching for whatever it is poets search for, and earning a living along the way on building sites and berry fields, fishing boats and drilling rigs, amassing the experience and imagery for which he is now known. Eventually this emerged in two pamphlets, *The Winter House*, 1982, then *Into The Anarchic* in 1985 when he was awarded a Scottish Arts Council Bursary. Keepdate Publishing produced *On the Rigs (1992)*, a collaboration with photographer Alan Wright of images from the North Sea oil field (1992). In 2004 *Scotia Review* published *Black Fish*, a pamphlet of recent poems.

While poetry is the basis of Gunn's work the theatre has always fascinated him. In 1982 he became joint coordinator of the ground-breaking Edinburgh Playwrights' Workshop. After stints with Scottish Youth Theatre and Eden Court Theatre, he set up the Grey Coast Theatre Company in 1992, based in Thurso, Caithness and is its current Artistic Director. Grey Coast has mounted over twenty productions, most recently *The Big Song Of Sutherland* and *Oedipus the Chief*, part one of a three-play cycle, *Oedipus North*. Its work ranges from national tours of plays by new Highland writers, schools work and community theatre, to collaboration with artists from Iceland, Ireland and Canada.

For Gunn, there can be no separation of poetry from theatre; both are mutually bound by cultural history and artistic desire. He is now adapting Neil Gunn's novel *Butcher's Broom* for a school production, working on a new book of poems, *The Atlantic Forest,* and has recently had poems translated into French.

He lives in Thurso with his partner Christine Russell, editor of *Scotia Review*, and is a Drama Tutor at North Highland College.

Chapman Books by George Gunn: (prices inc p & p)

Drama: Gold of Kildonan and *Songs of The Grey Coast*, 1992 – £8.95
Poetry: Sting, 1991 – £7.50;   *Whins,* 1996– £8.50

Whins has an intimate touch that runs like a golden seam through the book. Landscape and love come together, and a feeling of poignancy is delivered in the whole. There is a sense of loss all the more real for its transparency. This is possibly Gunn's best and subtlest work so far – Robert Davidson